Pronouns

by Katie Marsico

CHERRY LAKE PUBLISHING · ANN ARBOR, MICHIGAN

CHERRY LAKE
Publishing

Published in the United States of America by Cherry Lake Publishing
Ann Arbor, Michigan
www.cherrylakepublishing.com

Content Adviser: Lori Helman, PhD, Associate Professor, Department of
Curriculum & Instruction, University of Minnesota, Minneapolis, Minnesota

Photo Credits: Page 4, ©Levranii/Dreamstime.com; page 8, ©Monkey
Business Images/Shutterstock, Inc.; page 11, ©Brenda Carson/Shutterstock,
Inc.; page 16, ©MANDY GODBEHEAR/Shutterstock, Inc.; page 19,
©Sonya Etchison/Dreamstime.com; page 20, ©PhotoAlto/Alamy.

Library of Congress Cataloging-in-Publication Data
Marsico, Katie, 1980–
    Pronouns / By Katie Marsico.
        pages cm. — (Language Arts Explorer Junior)
    Includes bibliographical references and index.
    ISBN 978-1-62431-178-9 (lib. bdg.) — ISBN 978-1-62431-244-1
(e-book) — ISBN 978-1-62431-310-3 (pbk.)
    1. English language—Pronoun—Juvenile literature. I. Title.

PE1261. M37 2013
428.2—dc23   2013006092

Cherry Lake Publishing would like to acknowledge the work of The
Partnership for 21st Century Skills. Please visit *www.p21.org* for more
information.

Printed in the United States of America
Corporate Graphics Inc.
July 2013
CLFA13

A note on the text:
Certain words
are highlighted
as examples of
pronouns.

Bold, colorful
words are
vocabulary words
and can be found
in the glossary.

Table of Contents

CHAPTER ONE

Are They Here Yet?

Have you ever rolled out dough to make cookies?

Sam was thrilled that his cousins were coming to visit. He helped his mom bake cookies while he waited for them to arrive.

"Gosh, are they here yet?" Sam wondered aloud. He looked out the window. "I feel like I have not spent time with them in forever!"

"That is true," said his mom. "Their schedules have been crazy. You have not seen each other in a while."

"What should we do when they arrive, Mom?" Sam asked.

"Whatever you and your cousins want," she answered. "I think you should decide for yourselves. For starters, I hope you eat these delicious cookies. Would you like to try some now?"

Sam and his mom used **pronouns** to discuss his cousins' visit. Pronouns are words that substitute, or take the place of, a noun or noun **phrase**. Nouns and noun phrases identify a person, place, object, quality, or action.

OBJECTS IDEAS PLACES PEOPLE ANIMALS

The noun or noun phrase that a pronoun replaces is called the antecedent. The antecedent usually comes at some point before the pronoun in a text or conversation. Otherwise, it would not be clear what exactly a pronoun identified!

"Jim is my favorite cousin," said Sam. "He loves soccer just like me!" Here the pronoun *he* refers to the antecedent *Jim*.

Imagine if Sam never mentioned anyone's name: "He is my favorite cousin," said Sam. "He loves soccer just like me!" Without an antecedent, it is not clear to whom the pronoun *he* refers.

Who is he?

Extra Examples

Sam took a cookie. It was still hot.
Pronoun: it
Antecedent: cookie

Sam ate the cookie. Then he was full.
Pronoun: he
Antecedent: Sam

Sam's mom untied her apron.
Pronoun: her
Antecedent: Sam's mom

CHAPTER TWO

A Look at Pronouns

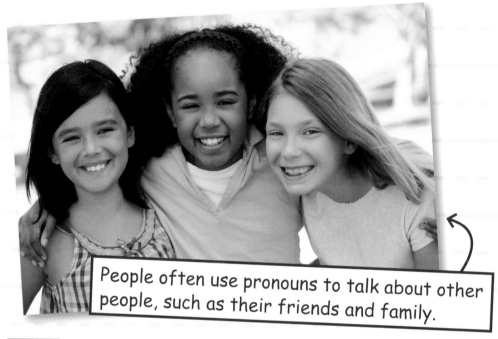

People often use pronouns to talk about other people, such as their friends and family.

"They are at the door!" yelled Sam. "Mom, I see them!"

"Go ahead and let your cousins in, Sam," his mom answered. "Please take their coats, too."

"Sam, how great to see you," his cousin Anna said. She gave Sam a big hug. Jim followed her inside.

"Hey, Sam," he shouted. "Do you have a hug for your other cousin?"

Many pronouns refer to a person, an **object**, or a group of people or objects. *I, me, we, us, you, he, she, him, her, it, they*, and *them* are personal pronouns. So are the words *mine, ours, yours, his, hers, its*, and *theirs*.

"This is going to be an awesome visit," said Anna. "What smells so good?"

"Those are cookies Mom and I made," replied Sam. Some pronouns point out the antecedent. *This* and *those* are two examples. For example, in Sam's sentence, *those* is the pronoun. *Cookies* is the antecedent. *That* and *these* are also used in this way.

To get a copy of this activity, visit www.cherrylakepublishing.com/activities.

STOP! DON'T WRITE IN THE BOOK!

ACTIVITY

Locate and List!

Locate and list all the pronouns in the following sentences:

"We ate lunch but are still starving," said Jim.

"That was hours ago," added Anna. "Besides, I always have room for Aunt Sara's desserts!"

"Those look delicious," Jim agreed. He stared at the cookies.

Answers: we, that, I, those, he

"The batch that we baked today is chocolate chip," said Sam's mom.

"I do not know anyone who turned down Aunt Sara's cookies," said Jim. Sometimes a pronoun begins a **clause**, or phrase, *that* gives more information about its antecedent. For example, the pronoun *that* refers to the noun *batch*. The pronoun leads a clause explaining what kind of cookie the batch is.

"I will help myself to a littlle snack," said Anna. Some pronouns refer back to a sentence's **subject**. The subject of a sentence is what performs the action in a sentence. Here, the subject is *I* and the action is *will help*. The pronoun *myself* refers back to the subject, *I*. Such pronouns are called reflexive. They show a subject is doing something to itself.

Pronouns are used to begin clauses that give extra details about something, including delicious cookies!

myself yourself ourselves itself herself himself themselves

Reflexive pronouns end in *-self* or *-selves*. They include *myself*, *ourselves*, *yourself*, *yourselves*, *himself*, *herself*, *itself*, and *themselves*. Removing reflexive pronouns changes a sentence's meaning or causes the sentence to no longer make sense. "I'll just help myself to some of those cookies" would become "I'll just help to some of those cookies."

"I myself love baking sugar cookies," announced Jim. Here, the pronoun *myself* is intensive. Intensive pronouns look like reflexive pronouns but have a different job. They add special importance to their antecedents. They are not necessary to the text. For example, try

To get a copy of this activity, visit www.cherrylakepublishing.com/activities.

STOP! DON'T WRITE IN THE BOOK!

ACTIVITY

Read and Rethink!

Read the following conversation. Pay attention to the pronouns in red. Label each one as reflexive or intensive. (Remember, you can remove an *intensive* pronoun without changing a sentence's meaning!):

"You yourselves would be able to make this recipe," said Sam's mom.

"We are not allowed to cook by ourselves," replied Anna.

"I do not bake by myself either," said Sam. "But these directions are simple enough for kids themselves to follow."

Answers: yourselves, intensive; ourselves, reflexive; myself, reflexive; themselves, intensive

removing the pronoun *myself* from Jim's statement above. The sentence becomes "I love baking cookies," which has the same meaning.

Everyone had finished eating. "What do you guys want to do now?" Sam asked. "Which game should we play?" Pronouns such as *what* and *which* ask a question. Other examples include *who*, *whom*, and *whose*.

"Let's kick the soccer ball to each other," Jim said to Sam. *Each other* refers to a shared action or **relationship**. *One another* is another pronoun that works this way.

"Does anyone else want to play?" asked Sam. "Everyone is welcome to join the game!" Some pronouns do not replace a specific antecedent listed nearby. *Anyone* and *everyone* are two examples. Sam was probably using *everyone* to refer to Anna and his mom. Yet he never mentioned their names when speaking. Other such pronouns include *all*, *each*, *fewer*, *many*, *none*, *one*, *some*, and *someone*.

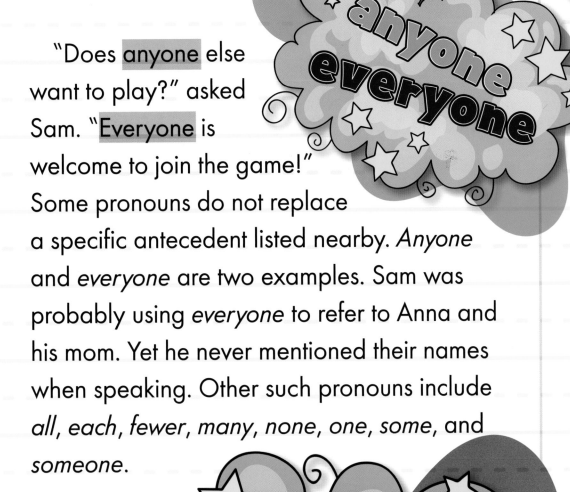

CHAPTER THREE

Recognize the Rules!

The goalie is one of the most important players on a soccer team.

"I was hoping you would say that!" remarked Anna. "Sam, do you want to know an interesting fact about me? I love soccer as much as Jim and you!"

"She is a great goalie," said Jim. "Her coach told me Anna is the best on her team, which is true!" Pronouns take different kinds of

Extra Example

"Anna is such an awesome player because she practices a lot," Jim added.

Here, both the antecedent (*Anna*) and the pronoun (*she*) are singular and female. Imagine how funny it would sound if the pronoun and antecedent did not agree. Would it make sense to say, "Anna is such an awesome player because they practices a lot"? Or "Anna is such an awesome player because he practices a lot"?

punctuation. They might come before or after commas. They can be followed by exclamation marks, question marks, and periods.

Yet people pay attention to more than punctuation when using pronouns. One important rule is that pronouns and their antecedents must "agree." They must match in qualities such as number and **gender**.

Another rule involves subject pronouns and object pronouns. People use subject pronouns when the pronoun is the subject of the sentence. The pronoun might also rename the subject of the sentence. Subject pronouns include *I*, *we*, *you*, *he*, *she*, *it*, and *they*. An object pronoun receives or is affected by the action of a verb. *Me*, *us*, *you*, *him*, *her*, *it*, and *them* are object pronouns.

THINK ABOUT IT

Extra Examples

"My soccer coach is amazing," said Anna. "He is so helpful!" Anna used the subject pronoun *he* because it is the subject of her second sentence.

"I like him, too," agreed Jim. Here, the object pronoun *him* is affected by the action *like*.

Playing sports is a great way to spend time with friends.

"We should start our soccer game soon," said Sam. "Anna and Jim, your parents are coming in about an hour. What do you want to do when we finish playing?"

"I think I know an activity everyone will enjoy," answered Anna. "How about treating ourselves to more cookies?"

Glossary

clause (KLAWZ) a group of words that contains a subject and a verb but is not a complete sentence

gender (JEN-dur) either of two groups consisting of male and female

object (AHB-jekt) a word or group of words that is affected by a verb

phrase (FRAYZ) a group of words that has a meaning but is not a sentence

pronouns (PRO-nownz) words that replace a noun or a noun phrase

punctuation (puhnk-chuh-WAY-shuhn) the marks used to separate words and sentences and help make their meaning clear

relationship (ri-LAY-shuhn-ship) the way in which two or more things are connected

subject (SUHB-jikt) a word or group of words in a sentence that tells who or what performs the action expressed by the verb

For More Information

BOOK

Doyle, Sheri. *What Is a Pronoun?* North Mankato, MN: Capstone Press, 2013.

WEB SITE

Iowa Public Television (IPTV)—Pronouns

www.iptv.org/kids/story.cfm/video/pbskids_20111111_pronouns/video

Check out a music video to learn more about pronouns!

Index

About the Author

Katie Marsico is the author of many children's and young-adult reference books. She lives outside of Chicago, Illinois, with her husband and children.